Simple Machines

Levers

Andrea Rivera

abdopublishing.com

Published by Abdo Zoom™, PO Box 398166, Minneapolis, Minnesota 55439. Copyright © 2017 by Abdo Consulting Group, Inc. International copyrights reserved in all countries. No part of this book may be reproduced in any form without written permission from the publisher. Abdo Zoom™ is a trademark and logo of Abdo Consulting Group, Inc.

Printed in the United States of America, North Mankato, Minnesota
102016
012017

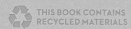

Cover Photo: Bahadir Tanriover/iStockphoto
Interior Photos: Bahadir Tanriover/iStockphoto, 1; Scand Photo/Shutterstock Images, 4; Joe Potato Photo/iStockphoto, 5; Morphart Creation/Shutterstock Images, 6–7; Shutterstock Images, 8, 12, 18; Andris Tkacenko/Shutterstock Images, 10; Jamie van Buskirk/iStockphoto, 11; Henk Badenhorst/iStockphoto, 13; Brent Hofacker/Shutterstock Images, 14; Sujitra Chaowdee/Shutterstock Images, 15; Fouad A. Saad/Shutterstock Images, 16–17; Christopher Futcher/iStockphoto, 21

Editor: Brienna Rossiter
Series Designer: Madeline Berger
Art Direction: Dorothy Toth

Publisher's Cataloging-in-Publication Data
Names: Rivera, Andrea, author.
Title: Levers / by Andrea Rivera.
Description: Minneapolis, MN : Abdo Zoom, 2017. | Series: Simple machines |
    Includes bibliographical references and index.
Identifiers: LCCN 2016949159 | ISBN 9781680799538 (lib. bdg.) |
    ISBN 9781624025396 (ebook) | ISBN 9781624025952 (Read-to-me ebook)
Subjects: LCSH: Levers—Juvenile literature.
Classification: DDC 621.8--dc23
LC record available at http://lccn.loc.gov/2016949159

Table of Contents

4

A lever is a **simple machine**.

It helps people
move heavy loads.

A bar goes under the load. A fulcrum supports the bar.

6

Pushing the bar
moves the load.

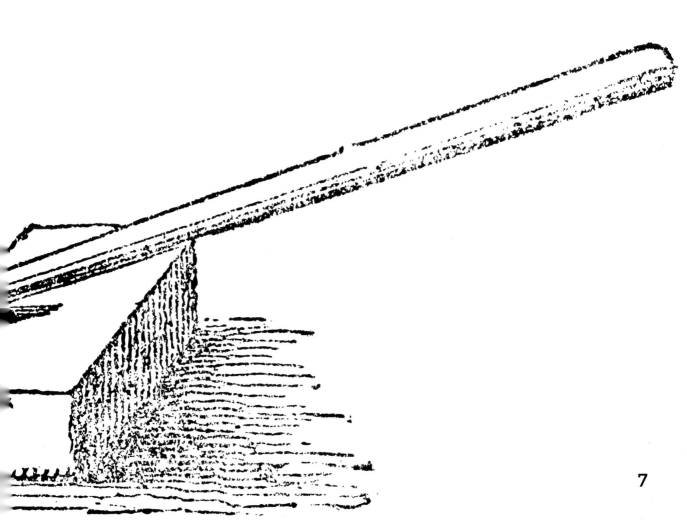

Technology

A load is at one end
of the lever.

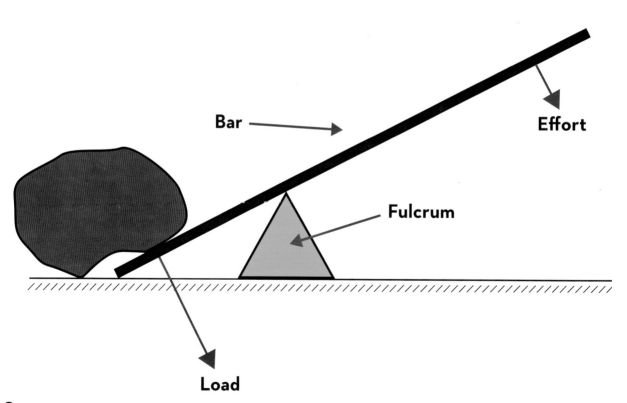

Bar

Effort

Fulcrum

Load

Effort is applied to the other end. The lever lifts the load.

Levers give a
mechanical advantage.

People can use
less force to move the load.

Engineering

A wheelbarrow uses a lever.
A load goes in the tray.

Force on the handles lifts it.
The wheel is the fulcrum.
It helps move the load, too.

Art

Nutcrackers use a lever.
You push on the lever.

This cracks the nut's shell.
Nutcrackers are painted
to look like people.

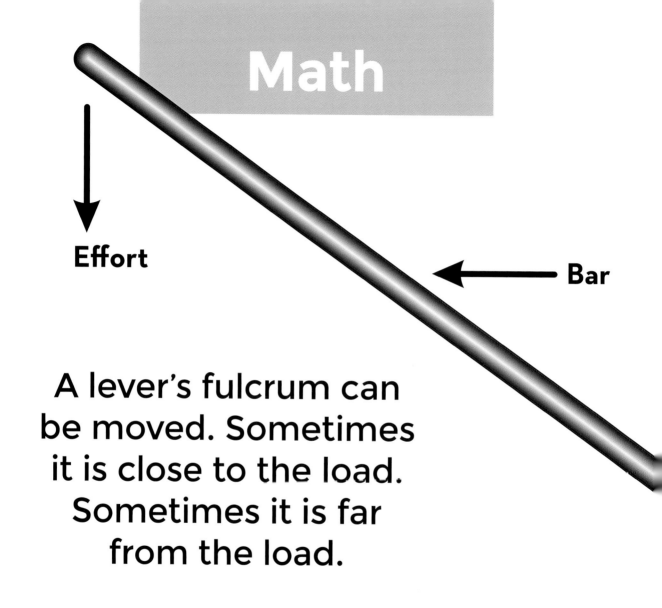

Effort

Bar

A lever's fulcrum can be moved. Sometimes it is close to the load. Sometimes it is far from the load.

16

Load

Fulcrum

17

Less force is needed when the fulcrum is closer to the load. You need less force if the fulcrum is 6 inches (0.15 m) from the load than if it is 16 inches (0.41 m) from the load.

- We use levers every day. When you open a door, you are using a lever. Scissors and brooms are levers, too.

- A baseball bat is another type of lever. A person's hands are the fulcrum.

- Ancient people used levers. Archimedes was a Greek mathematician. He was the first person to write about a lever. This happened around 260 BCE.

Glossary

effort - a force applied to a simple machine. A force is a push or pull that causes a change in motion.

fulcrum - the point on which a lever rests when it is lifting something.

load - an object that needs to be turned, lifted, or moved.

mechanical advantage - the way a simple machine makes work easier.

simple machine - a basic device that makes work easier.

Booklinks

For more information
on levers, please visit
booklinks.abdopublishing.com

Learn even more with the Abdo Zoom
STEAM database. Check out
abdozoom.com for more information.

Index